Foxes

Written by Jo Windsor

Rigby

Look at this animal.
This animal is a fox.
A fox can look like a dog.
This fox has a long nose.
It has a long
bushy tail, too.

bushy tail

long nose

This fox lives in the hot desert.
It has big, big ears.
The ears help the fox
keep cool.

The fox has fur
under its paws.
The fur helps keep
its paws cool.

big ears

This fox lives in the snow.
It has fur under its paws.
The fur helps keep
its paws warm.

Some foxes sleep
in the day.
They get their food
at night.

This fox likes
to eat birds.

Baby foxes are called cubs.
They are born in dens.
A den keeps cubs safe.
Some dens are
under the ground.
Some dens are in rocks.
Some dens
are in trees, too.

A mother fox can take
her cubs from den to den.
She takes them
in her mouth.

One day the cubs will be big.
They will be good
at getting their own food.
They will leave
the mother fox.

Index

Guide Notes

Title: Foxes
Stage: Early (3) – Blue

Genre: Nonfiction (Expository)
Approach: Guided Reading
Processes: Thinking Critically, Exploring Language, Processing Information
Written and Visual Focus: Photographs (static images), Labels, Captions, Index
Word Count: 164

THINKING CRITICALLY
(sample questions)
- Look at the front cover and the title. Ask the children: "What do you think this book could be about?"
- Ask the children what they know about foxes.
- Focus the children's attention on the Index. Ask: "What are you going to find out about in this book?"
- If you want to find out about getting food, on which pages would you look?
- If you want to find out about ears, on which page would you look?
- If you want to find out about cubs, on which page would you look?
- Look at pages 2 and 3. How does a fox look like a dog?
- What is different about the fox that lives in the desert and the fox that lives in the snow?
- Why do you think some dens are under the ground?

EXPLORING LANGUAGE

Terminology
Title, cover, photographs, author, photographers

Vocabulary
Interest words: bushy, desert, paws, cubs, dens
High-frequency words (new): long, keep, day, getting
Positional words: in, under

Print Conventions
Capital letter for sentence beginnings, periods, commas